Hugo Williams was born in Windsor in 1942 and grew up in Sussex. He worked on the *London Magazine* from 1961 to 1970, since when he has earned his living as a journalist and travel writer. He has been TV critic and poetry editor on the *New Statesman*, theatre critic on the *Sunday Correspondent* and film critic for *Harper's & Queen*. He writes the 'Freelance' column in the *TLS* and divides his time between London and France.

D0829679

Billy's Rain   HUGO WILLIAMS

faber and faber
LONDON·NEW YORK

First published in 1999
by Faber and Faber Limited
3 Queen Square London WC1N 3AU
Published in the United States by Faber and Faber, Inc.,
a division of Farrar, Straus and Giroux, Inc., New York

Photoset by Wilmaset Ltd, Wirral
Printed in England by MPG Books Limited,
Victoria Square, Bodmin, Cornwall

A CIP record for this book
is available from the British Library

ISBN 0–571–20086–9

Some of these poems first appeared in the *Independent on Sunday,
London Magazine, London Quarterly, London Review of Books,
Observer, Printer's Devil, Times Literary Supplement*, 'The Seven Deadly
Sins' (a Brighton Festival booklet) and 'Some R&B and Black Pop'
(Greville Press pamphlet).

I would like to thank Mary-Kay Wilmers and Neil Rennie for their
support – H.W.

10 9 8 7 6 5 4 3 2 1

Contents

Billy's Rain

Silver Paper Men

They exist in rudimentary gardens,
flourishing a cane or twirling a parasol,
all nipped-in waists, doffed hats
and little pointed shoes.
Regency bucks and belles,
they appear out of nowhere, for no reason,
leaning by a bridge or balustrade,
admiring a willow tree.
Given over to reflection,
they do nothing for a season, in pairs,
while a butterfly waits in mid-air.
That impossible basket of flowers
says all there is to say about love
in their shiny black world.

After dark, their silver paper costumes
shimmer in the light from the street.
Their flickering afterimages
stiff-leg-it round the room
in time to some tinselly tune from long ago.
For a moment, they seem to dance together.
Suddenly bashful, they hide
behind fans or dance programmes,
or turn their heads to one side.
They pass their days like this,
bowing and scraping to one another
on either side of a mantelpiece or door,
till one of them goes missing,
or crashes to the floor.

Trivia

It might have been the word for sulking in animals,
Juliette Lewis, Joan of Arc, the smell
of television lingering in the morning like a quarrel.
It might have been an Airedale scratching at your door,
papier-mâché heads, a cloud no bigger than ...

It might have been blue satin, Peter Stuyvesant Gold,
Deep Heat, umbrella pines, familiar two-note calls
repeated at intervals, a lifeguard's upraised hand.
It didn't matter what it was, almost anything would do
to bring it all back to you, then take it away again.

Day Return

Your thoughts race ahead of you down the line
to where the day is building
a strange new town for you to arrive in:
the ruined castle,
the different-coloured buses,
the girl from the office
who tears up your day return
and throws it in pieces at your feet.

You smile for no reason
at a cut-out of two workmen
carrying a ladder across a field
on behalf of 'KARPIN BROS REMOVALS AND DECORATIONS'.
Even the horses looking up from grass
seem to agree that time and you
are flying past for once
without knowing why exactly.

Sealink

On the boat, we foot passengers
were shuffled like a pack of cards
and thrown down in new combinations
all over the half-empty, off-season decks.
Children bumped into one another.
Parents looked for somewhere quiet to sit
away from the video games.
Young couples ate enormous, nervous meals,
while single people roamed back and forth
between the restaurant and Duty Free.

As land came into sight, one asked another
'Do you know the way back to the coach?
I think it's on Whale Deck.'
A conversation begins with 'May I sit
next to you? God, it's hot in here!
Do you mind if I open this window?'
We take off our coats, settle back, peel oranges.
Shall we speak in English or French?
Are we going on holiday? Or home?
Do we mind knowing each other's name?

Straw Dogs

When she says I have the gift of the gab
her dress is off the shoulder,
her breath is warm on my cheek. I talk so fast
about my brother's films and friends

I grow hoarse shouting their first names
over the Rolling Stones.
'STRAW DOGS' I yell to the room
as the music stops unexpectedly.

My Chances

As I grew warmer
and the bus went over the bumps,
I let my mind wander
further and further,
checking my scowl
in the window of the bus
against my chances
of bending her over that table,
the arm of that chair.

When she answered the door
in her low-cut dress
I forgot what it was
I was going to do to her.
I gave her a kiss
and asked if she was ready to go out,
checking my smile
in the mirror in the hall
against my chances of being liked.

Till Soon

How I laughed at your orders.
I shall obey them to the letter,
not forgetting the short-back-and-sides
and the shirt that isn't button-down.
I agree with you about the car.
Why suffer when we can travel in comfort?
Just let the weather be fine,
but it doesn't matter what it's like
so long as we can walk around together
and make fun of everything,
the way we did last time.

Interval

Scene shifters have come on
under cover of dark,
anonymous creatures
in soft shoes and black pullovers,
who move about the stage
with easy familiarity,
scattering magazines,
resetting the hands of a clock.

They change the position of a lamp
or piece of furniture,
butting it with a hip,
nudging it into the future.
A couple of cushions on the floor,
the angle of a sofa,
are all we need to know
about a missing hour.

During an Absence

Now that she has left the room for a moment
to powder her nose,
we watch and wait, watch and wait,
for her to bring back the purpose into our lives.

How

How you fell asleep in your chair
and woke up some time later
and said, 'It's hot in here'
and asked for a glass of water.

How you stretched out your hand for the glass
and a look came into your eye
which might have been laziness
or might have been lechery.

Collarbone

Your hair hacked close to your head
by someone calling herself a friend,
the gap in your teeth, the squint,
the grown-up, own-up evening gown,
the delicate collarbone
you would one day fall and break.

The fracture was serious enough
to require two pins – a crooked line of stitches
where I had kissed you.
Only three days after the operation
you wanted to go to bed
and only cried out once.

Timer

The smell of ammonia in the entrance hall.
The racing bike. The junk mail.
The timer switch whose single naked bulb
allowed us as far as the first floor.
The backs of your legs
as you went ahead of me up the stairs.

The landing where we paused for breath
and impatient key searching.
The locks which would never open quickly enough
to let us in.
The green of the paintwork we slid down
as if we had nowhere else to go.

Nothing On

Alone at last
and plastered from the mini-bar
we were looking around
for something to amuse us
in the hotel room
when you fell upon
the Gideon Bible
in the bedside table
and made me read to you
from the Book of Genesis.

If you carry on
dancing round the room like that
in your sun-tan swim-suit
twirling the hotel's
complimentary fruitbowl
it won't be long
till the page fills up
with four-letter words
and I lose my place
in the story of the Creation.

Rhetorical Questions

How do you think I feel
when you make me talk to you
and won't let me stop
till the words turn into a moan?
Do you think I mind
when you put your hand over my mouth
and tell me not to move
so you can 'hear' it happening?

And how do you think I like it
when you tell me what to do
and your mouth opens
and you look straight through me?
Do you think I mind
when the blank expression comes
and you set off alone
down the hall of collapsing columns?

The Lisboa

Pass me the alarm clock, Carolyn.
What time do you have to go to work?
I'll set it for half past seven,
then we'll have time for breakfast.
I'll get the milk.

Listen, why don't you ring up in the morning
and say you're going to be late?
Then we can do what we like.
We could go to the Lisboa and have custard tarts.
We could go to the Gate.

Lift up your arms.
Let me take this off.

Our Theory

Though working out of
different locations
too much of the time
on one occasion at least
we arrived at
similar conclusions.

Your voice on the phone
had been outlining
a theory of displacement
hingeing on a single
practical experiment
you were performing.

I hung on the line
excitedly roughing out
my response to your ideas
all fingers and thumbs
as I let my thoughts pour out
on a blank sheet.

Billy's Rain

When I'm lying awake, listening to rain
hammering on the roof,
the phrase comes back to me,
our code for 'Let's get out of here'.
We were huddled in the back of a van
with the lights, the videotape equipment
and the man with the rain machine.
'Why can't we use the regular rain?' you asked,
as rain hammered on the roof.
'That's God's rain,' said someone.
'It doesn't show up on film.
We need Billy's rain for this one.'
When I find myself soaked to the skin, tired,
or merely bored with God's rain,
the phrase comes back to me.
I'd say it now if I thought you were listening.

Cross Country

The train drivels north in a series
of false starts and broken promises,
pauses for thought alongside a giant blonde.
Only another hour till I see you,
running down the platform to meet me.
I don't think I can wait that long.

Everywhere I look, little passionate scenes
are being played out against a background
of hurrying clouds. Every couple I see
fills me with insane jealousy.
What does she see in him?
What does he see in her?
Why is love between other people so tender and pure?

At Euston Station I found myself standing next to a man
with the same overnight bag as me,
looking at the same middle-aged woman
who smoothed her jumper over low-slung breasts.
I was so excited I got on the train before mine,
a sadistic 'Cross Country' affair
which dawdles between stations, making me beg for it.

Here's a woman I already feel close to
after only half an hour
of trying not to look at her bare arms.
She lifts them above her head
in a gesture of boredom or surrender.
Her hands touch in mid-air and she turns them
inside out in a kind of question mark.
I'm carrying my head on a platter.
If I make a move I'll probably spill myself.

Late

By the time we limp into Manchester
half an hour late, the moment has been lost
when I might have passed myself off
as myself. I wave as usual,

but you look straight through me,
searching other faces in the crowd
for someone you thought you would recognise
if you ever saw him again.

Lost Weekend

The hotel cost too much
so we didn't even touch the bed
and said we'd decided
not to take it after all

and just picked up our things
and set off down the road
till we came to this youth hostel
in an old hospital

and asked ourselves quietly
what we were doing there
and laid out the remains of the picnic
and took stock of the situation.

Get that chair over there
and we'll just sit here and talk.
It's been a long day. Our feet hurt.
Our money is running out.

When I've calmed down a bit
I'll go out and see if I can find such a thing
as a bottle of wine
in this godforsaken town.

Among the Combs

Among the combs and face creams
of her childhood sponge-bag,
tangled with her hair –
the green-and-silver blister pack
marked with the days of the week.

We follow the arrows printed on the pack
and move around clockwise.
The days fly past in an endless stream,
leaving only a rip in the tinfoil
and nothing in the world to fear.

At the Brief Encounter

Five minutes left to go in this pink-shot
station café, being stared at by a boy.
What shall we do? What shall we say?

I know. Let's cry. Let's scream.
Let's tear down the station with our bare hands.
Let's scatter it to the four winds.

Token

For I am sorry about what happened at the fairground the
other day.

For I regret not going on any of the rides.

For I am sending this token of my resolution to do better
next time, if there is a next time.

For I undertake to escort the holder on the Big Dipper, the
Golden Galloper, the Chair-O-Plane, the Wagon Wheel
and anything else she wants to go on.

For that includes the Whip, the Pirate Ship, the Surf Dancer
and the Wind Runner.

For I also promise to accompany her on the Underwater
Adventure.

For I further guarantee not to chicken out of the Crater.

For I am willing to enter the Haunted House, if she will go
in with me.

For I am even willing to go on the Bumping Cars, which
proves how much I love her.

For if all this fails to please her I will grow a pair of wings
for the occasion and fly with her across the sky.

Last Things

They must be checking our location on the map,
taking leave of their loved ones,
asking the way to our house.

They are not in any hurry to get here.
They have a certain schedule to stick to.
They know where we are.

If we try to see them, outlined against the horizon,
they stand completely still, looking innocent.
If we turn our backs on them, they move
forward again, more confident.

One evening, when nothing much is going on,
they detach themselves from the surrounding countryside
and begin their advance across no-man's-land.
They make themselves known to us
in a ripple of ill-wind.

Lunch Hour

On a traffic island
  buses sway the flowers
    people trot across

Some stay on the seat
  light a cigarette
    unfold their newspapers

Sun is out all day
  shining on metal
    we sit on the wall

Astonishing how similar
  minute by minute
    dream you are fine

All Right

I'm lying awake somewhere between
the yellow pilot-light
of the Dimplex thermostat
and the winking eye of the fax,
making the journey across town,
past all the stations in North London,
going over Bishop's Bridge,
entering the badlands.

I hear your giggles as I hit the bumps
in the curved section
of Westbourne Park Road.
I see the crack of light in your curtains
when I stop at the lights
at the corner of Ladbroke Grove.
If you go past your window now
everything will be all right.

Rainy Night

Something about the hiss of a taxi
cruising an empty street,
its foggy yellow light
skidding off piles of black bin-liners
is trying to let me know
this isn't my night.

Something about the look of your front door,
its familiar fanlight star
picked out in black
is trying to get through to me
that you and I
have turned some sort of corner.

Rain off the river, mixed with the smell
of pavements in summer,
is trying to let me down lightly.
I stand on the step
while the sound of your doorbell
echoes down the hall.

Their Holidays

Striped light coming through the blinds
and falling on the bed
where the man and woman are kneeling.

I don't know what they are doing.
I don't really care.
I said, 'Hello, what are you doing here?'

I was standing in the middle of the room
trying to make a telephone call.
I kept taking the receiver off the hook

and putting it back again.
I moved forward, to where I would remain,
standing at the foot of the bed.

It was something like a dog and bitch
who craned their necks around,
striped light coming through the blinds.

Dangerous Water

Don't go over there, Carolyn,
past the nightclub, past the boats, past the rocks,
where the waves come furthest up the beach
in natural swimming pools.

It's deserted over there now,
except for one or two fishermen and one or two couples
looking for a place to be alone.
I don't like to think of you over there.

I don't like to think of you
when the tide suddenly turns
and the sun goes down behind the town.
You could get cut off over there, as we should know.

And don't try to swim for it, the way you did last time.
Wait till I get there.
Then we'll have to spend the night together
in the old Rasta Bar.

Strange Meeting

I ring up in the usual way,
but something's not quite right.
Instead of saying 'Hello, how are you?
Can you come out to play?'
she suggests 'meeting up' some time,
which makes my blood run cold.
I'm on my way round there now
with flowers and other apologies.

For a moment the doorbell excites me
with scenes out of the past,
but the kiss on both cheeks
and the cheerful look on her face
as she takes my coat for me
are pointers to a brand new future
she ushers me into now
and asks me to sit down.

Nothing Stinted

We have taken up our positions
over a complicated board game
of coffee, cigarettes, wine
(nothing stinted for the occasion)
while she tells me with a certain sadness
how she's got 'muddled up' with her boss.

I come out of my corner laughing, likeable,
full of stories about my trip.
I refill her glass for her.
Feigning concern for her welfare
and knowing her openness on the subject,
I ask about birth control.
What method are they using?
Are they being careful?

She leans towards me across the table.
'Remember you used to tell me
men would always treat me badly if I let them?
Well, he doesn't. He treats me well.
You don't have to worry about that.'

Congratulations

It looks at first like a horse
failing repeatedly to clear a fence,
rearing up, stalling for a moment,
sinking down between her thighs.
I watch from my vantage point
as she urges him on with her heel.
Given that sort of encouragement,
and seeing the look on her face,
I feel sure I would make a better job
of surmounting such an obstacle,
but there's no getting away from the fact
that she finds his efforts acceptable,
even, now that he is sprawled all
over her, worthy of congratulation.

Unobtainable

Whether it was putting in an extra beat
or leaving one out, I couldn't tell.
My heart seemed to have forgotten
everything it ever knew
about timing and co-ordination
in its efforts to get through to someone
on the other side of a wall.
As I lay in bed, I could hear it
hammering away inside my pillow,
being answered now and then
by a distant guitar-note of bedsprings,
pausing for a moment, as if listening,
then hurrying on as before.

Alternator

To be in possession of the facts, yet powerless,
is new to me, a strange technology
of waiting, hanging by a thread,
watching the dud decisions
fizzing and popping in the night,
like this moth-crazed street light,
its opposite poles rigged to an alternator
of breaking up or asking her to marry me.

I make my heart beat, remembering her silences.
My brains fly out through the top of my head.
Run to the ends of the earth?
Or set up camp on her doorstep?
I take my place on her answering tape.
My innocent enquiries. My carefree messages.
'The phone was ringing when I came in ...
I was wondering if you'd got my letter ...'

Blindfold Games

It isn't so much that he loves her
and wants to marry her
that keeps me awake at night
as the thought of them stumbling upstairs together
in a sort of three-legged race.

I only have to close my eyes
and he is taking her by the arm,
pushing her towards the bedroom.
He has left the door half open,
but I can't quite see what they are doing,
only glimpses from time to time,
the backs of her legs, the scar on her shoulder.

I turn to look away,
but the shock of her pleasure rises in my throat,
the insult of her sweat mingling with his sweat,
her saying certain things,
her throwing out one arm.

Live Bed Show

For I notice it isn't me
bumping so realistically against her thighs,
leaning forward, whispering in her ear
unscripted obscenities.
For I remember playing the same part myself
in another lifetime.
For those were the days
when she and I never tired
of improvising fresh pieces of action.
For we thought and acted as one.

For I notice it isn't me
rising above her now, simulating climax.
For I have to admit
she enters into the spirit of the thing
with uncanny conviction.
For I keep reminding myself
that nothing is really happening between them.
For it seems so unlikely somehow.
For I must be imagining things.
For I take some comfort from this.

Sweet Nothings

Not her mouth not her chin not her throat.
Not her smell not her skin not her sweat.

No laughs and no jokes and no thoughts.
No words and no desires – none of that any more.

None of that any more and all of it still.
All of it still and more and more of it every day.

All That

And then there's the one you write
that makes even you laugh.
You never want to see her again.
You don't want to see her handwriting
on a letter. You don't want to come home
and see the little yellow light
flashing messages of regret.
You don't want to pick up the phone
and hear how much she's been missing you.
Couldn't you meet for a drink?
Not any more. Maybe in a year or two.
All you want to do now
is draw a line under your life
and get on with the past.
Do you make yourself perfectly clear?
You sign with just your name,
a businesslike touch
which makes even you laugh.

Haircut

How idiotic two months later
the hair curling over my collar
the fringe falling in my eyes
as I catch a glimpse in the mirror
of the haircut she arranged
the haircut she supervised
its stupidity its ignorance its bliss.

How I envy my last haircut
that knows nothing of all this
that cannot hear her voice
laughing and apologising
for the haircut by her friend
the haircut that would soon grow out
its innocence its happiness its peace.

Useless

I narrowed it down to this –
her voice on the phone,
its cheerful 'Hello, how are you?
Can you come out to play?'
I wrapped her choking laugh
in layers of indifference.
I couldn't get rid of her mouth.

I narrowed it down once more –
a look on her face,
one arm across my neck.
As a final test
I allowed her to speak my name.
That was no good at all.
That was worse than useless.

Erosion

The cricketer proves my theory
of erosion, landslide, wilderness.
He teetered on the brink
of a difficult decision,
before coming down firmly
on the dining-room floor.

I almost caught him –
or did I give him a little push?
At any rate, he slipped through my fingers,
somersaulted once or twice
and made his eloquent last point
from all over the place.

Mirror History

Round about here I become aware of your
existence for the first time, that you might even
be alive, in the sense that I am alive,
walking around having thoughts about everything,
but keeping a pleasant expression on your face.
I wonder why it never struck me before
that you might not be happy all the time.

When I think about lovemaking for instance
it occurs to me that you might not have been
faking it after all, that perhaps it was me
who was putting on an act for your benefit.
As if you couldn't read me like a book!
How strange to think there were two of us
doing those things and I never realised.

Re-reading what I have written up till now
I am conscious only of what is not being said,
the mirror history running underneath all this
self-pitying nonsense. To hear me talk
you'd think I was the aggrieved party,
whereas we both know it was my own decision
to do nothing that made nothing happen.

Even as we were breaking up for the last time
I was looking at my watch behind your back,
thinking: what shall we do next? Through my tears
I made out the hands telling me I was late
for something or other, so I cut short my visit
and went dashing off across London on the bike,
telling myself I could always go back if I wanted to.

If only they were waiting for us somewhere,
the nights we didn't use, the things we didn't do,
the bridge we didn't lean on in the moonlight,
watching the barges pass beneath our feet.
Instead, a faint glimmer appears on the horizon,
as if someone were signalling through mist.
A ghost with a yellow shopping bag
waves to a yellow raincoat
at the other end of a street.

Some R&B and Black Pop

I refused to say anything
when Charlie and Inez Foxx sang 'Mockingbird',
or Oscar Wills sang 'Flat Foot Sam'.
I remained silent throughout Elmore James's version
of 'Stormy Monday'. I didn't give in
to Gene Allison or Sonny Boy Williamson.

I broke down and admitted everything
when I reached the place on the tape
where Lazy Lester's 'I'm a Lover Not a Fighter'
suddenly gets much louder
and one of us always had to get out of bed
to turn the volume down.

Blank Pages

This is the room
where we struggled with the words to your songs,
disjointed, two-note things
which seemed to have no refrains,

or lay awake in the same bed,
hearing our verses crackling all night
in the waste-paper basket:
paper flesh, blood ink.

The deadline came round
like a vast tick of the clock.
The minute hand moved on with a little jerk.
We laid aside our work.

And then the blank pages
at the end of an old notebook,
left behind in a suitcase,
taking up too much room under the stairs.

I'm writing in it now –
disjointed scenes from our life,
its early promise, personal triumphs,
eventual loss of faith.

How I held the door for you,
in ignorance of love,
dragging you back again too late to save the day.
How I did the same thing twice.

It sounds like one of our songs –
the dry laughter of tearing paper,
the sensation of falling,
of falling through the tear.

Early Morning

Each dawn might be peacetime again –
white empty skies, the glow of battle
turned to ash-coloured light.

For a little while longer
opposing forces sleep.
The linings of curtains look like flags of surrender.

A cry of pleasure is followed by a baby's cry.
Without this truce each day
God knows where we would be.

a

tiful it would be to wait for you again
al place,
ng at the door,
 lookout in the long mirror,
hat if you are late
 be too late,
 hat all I have to do
ittle longer
ill be pushing through the other customers,
ath, apologetic.
e you been, for God's sake?
ing to worry.

 did we say we would wait
s was held up?
o long and still no sign of you.
es by, I search other faces in the bar,
g their features
are monstrous versions of you,
s wobbling from side to side
 on sticks.
nce inches forward
tanding next to me.
s taken the seat I was saving.
re face to face in the long mirror.

Everyone Knows This

How am I feeling this mornin
Or is it too early to say?
I check by swallowing
to see if my throat's still sore
I check by thinking
to see if my brain still hurts.

I'm walking along out of doo
not feeling anything much,
when it suddenly comes to n
I don't feel so bad any more
I think to myself,
'I'll soon put a stop to that!'

Bar Ital

How bea
in the us
not look
keeping
knowing
it will n
knowing
is wait a
and you
out of br
Where h
I was sta

How lon
if one of
It's been
As time g
rearrangi
until they
their heac
like heads
Your abs
until it is
Now it h
Now we

Legend

X's darken the map of London
in the places we made love.
Footprints hurry back and forth
from Chelsea to Ladbroke Grove.

Winged hearts accompany our progress.
Flaming arrows signify intent.
Grappling hooks are loving glances.
Handcuffs are kindly meant.

Knives and forks are for dining out.
Wine glasses are for romancing.
Skeletons mark the Latin American clubs
where we used to go dancing.

Siren Song

I phone from time to time, to see if she's
changed the music on her answerphone.
'Tell me in two words,' goes the recording,
'what you were going to tell in a thousand.'

I peer into that thought, like peering out
to sea at night, hearing the sound of waves
breaking on rocks, knowing she is there,
listening, waiting for me to speak.

Once in a while she'll pick up the phone
and her voice sings to me out of the past.
The hair on the back of my neck stands up
as I catch her smell for a second.

Her News

You paused for a moment and I heard you smoking
on the other end of the line.
I pictured your expression,
one eye screwed shut against the smoke
as you waited for my reaction.
I was waiting for it myself, a list of my own news
gone suddenly cold in my hand.
Supposing my wife found out, what would happen then?
Would I have to leave her and marry you now?

Perhaps it wouldn't be so bad,
starting again with someone new, finding a new place,
pretending the best was yet to come.
It might even be fun,
playing the family man, walking around in the park
full of righteous indignation.
But no, I couldn't go through all that again,
not without my own wife being there,
not without her getting cross about everything.

Perhaps she wouldn't mind about the baby,
then we could buy a house in the country
and all move in together.
That sounded like a better idea.
Now that I'd been caught at last, a wave of relief
swept over me. I was just considering
a shed in the garden with a radio and a day bed,
when I remembered I hadn't seen you for over a year.
'Congratulations,' I said. 'When's it due?'

Balcony Scene

The street light shorting on and off,
casting a balcony on my bedroom wall.
I seem to have wired it up
to my thoughts of you, your first-floor studio,
the ladder to your bed, car lights overhead.

I was climbing the ladder one night
when I caught the eye of a man
going past on the top of a bus
and for one moment became him
as he turned to look back at us.
I fell asleep after that, never dreaming
I would give it a second thought.

I see his face now, passing my window,
as I draw the curtains for the night,
the street light shorting on and off,
somehow refusing to blow.